THE PRINCIPLES OF WEALTH ACCRETION

LEARN WHY & HOW TO MAKE THE MONEY, THEN CREATE THE RULES!

Contents

The Prime Directives of Wealth Acquisition 2

The fact is, many people think they understand economy when they really do not. 3

DON'T MISS YOUR OPPORTUNITY 11

RIGHT PLACE, RIGHT TIME 12

AVOID DEBT LIKE THE PLAGUE 13

SELF-RELIANCE IS REALLY JUST ANOTHER WORD FOR PERSEVERENCE. 14

WHATEVER YOU DO, DO IT WITH ALL YOUR MIGHT 16

USE YOUR OWN PERSONAL EXERCISES AS A GUIDE. 17

USE THE BEST TOOLS 19

DON'T GET ABOVE YOUR BUSINESS 20

LEARN SOMETHING VALUE-ADDED 23

LEAD WITH HOPE, BUT DON'T BE TOO VISIONARY 24

BE SYSTEMATIC 24

DON'T DISTRIBUTE YOUR POWERS 25

READ THE DAILY PAPERS 26

DON'T INDORSE WITHOUT SECURITY 26

BE POLITE AND KIND TO YOUR CUSTOMERS 29

BE CHARITABLE 29

PRESERVE YOUR INTEGRITY 30

REMOVE BLAB 32

The Prime Directives of Wealth Acquisition

The ability to earn money is not at all difficult for those in excellent health in the United States, since there is more land than people. Any individual of either sex who is willing, at least temporarily, to engage in any respectable activity that offers may find successful work in this fairly new sector since there are so many opportunities for success open and so many uncrowded occupations.

Those who genuinely want independence merely need to make up their minds to do so and use the appropriate methods, just as they would for any other goal they intend to achieve. However simple it may be to generate money, I'm sure many of my listeners will agree that maintaining it is the hardest thing in the world. As Dr. Franklin accurately states, "the road to wealth is as plain as the road to the mill." It just involves spending less than we make; that seems like a fairly straightforward issue. To have an annual income of twenty pounds and spend twenty pounds and sixpence is to be the most miserable of men, while to have an income of only twenty pounds and spend only nineteen pounds and sixpence is to be the happiest of mortals, according to Mr. Micawber, one of those happy creations of the genial Dickens. Many of my readers could respond, "We get it; this is economics, and we know economics is wealth; we know we can't have our cake and eat it, too. However, more failures may result from errors on this issue than practically any other.

The fact is, many people think they understand economy when they really do not.

The concept of true economy is misunderstood, and as a result, many individuals live their lives without fully understanding it. One person complains, "I make so much money, and here is my neighbor who makes the same; yet every year he comes out ahead and I fall short. I am well-versed in economics. He believes he does, but he is mistaken. Some guys believe that being frugal involves doing all sorts of tiny, nasty, dirty things like saving cheese parings and candle ends, taking two pence off the laundress' fee, etc. Economics is not a cruel thing. Additionally, these group of people made the unfortunate decision to solely use their economy in one direction. They believe they are so amazingly frugal that they can afford to waste money in other areas since they saved a half-penny when they should have spent two pennies.

Before kerosene oil was found or even considered, one might spend the night at practically any farmer's house in the agricultural areas and have a very fine dinner, but thereafter, he would try to read in the living room but would find it difficult due to the inefficient light of one candle. Upon observing his predicament, the hostess would respond: "It is really difficult to read here in the evenings; the saying goes, "You must have a ship at sea in order to be able to light two candles at once; we never have an additional candle except on extra occasions." These extra events happen maybe twice a year. In this way the good woman saves five, six, or ten dollars in that time: but the information which might be derived from having the extra light would, of course, far outweigh a ton of candles.

But this is not the end of the problem. She believes that because she is so frugal with tallow candies, she can afford to frequent the town and spend $20–$30 on ribbons and furbelows, many of which are unnecessary. Men in business may regularly exhibit this erroneous connotation, and in those cases, the first thing they go for is writing paper. Good businessmen will conserve all the used envelopes and paper scraps and, if at all possible, will not rip a fresh sheet of paper. They may save five or ten dollars a year in this way, which is great, but because they are so frugal (just with note paper), they believe they can afford to spend time, have lavish parties, and drive their carriages. This is an example of Dr. Franklin's adage, "penny smart and pound foolish," or "saving at the spigot and spending at the bung-hole." "They are like the man who purchased a penny herring for his family's dinner and then hired a coach and four to take it home," Punch in remarks in reference to this "one idea" kind of individuals. I've never heard of an individual who achieved success through this sort of economics.

True economics involves constantly ensuring that revenue exceeds expenditures. Wear the old clothing a little longer if necessary; forgo the new pair of gloves; fix the old outfit; live on simpler food if required; this way, under any circumstances, unless an unexpected accident occurs, there will be a margin in favor of the income. The intended outcome is accomplished by placing a penny here and a dollar there at interest, which continues to accumulate. This economy may need some training, but if you get acclimated to it, you'll discover that logical saving gives you more happiness than impulsive spending.

I suggest making the following recipe: **It is, in my experience, a fantastic remedy for excess, particularly for misguided economics**. If you discover that you don't have any extra money at the end of the year while making a nice wage, I suggest that you take a few sheets of paper, bind them into a book, and list every expense. You will see that the latter column will be double, triple, and even ten times bigger than the former if you post it every day or week in two columns, one entitled "necessaries" or even "comforts," and the other headed "luxuries." Real creature luxuries are quite inexpensive compared to what the majority of us can make. We are not destroyed by our own eyes, but rather by those of others. I wouldn't care about expensive clothing or furniture if everyone else in the world were blind but me. We are all free and equal is a phrase that many people in America like to repeat, but it is a grave error in more ways than one. That we are born "free and equal" is a glorious truth in one sense, yet we are not all born equally rich, and we never shall be.

It is possible to say, "There is a man who makes $50,000 per year while I only make $1,000; I knew that fellow when he was poor like myself; now that he is rich and thinks he is better than I am; I will prove to him that I am as good as he is; I will go and buy a horse and buggy; no, I cannot do that; but I will go and hire one and ride this afternoon on the same road that he does."

My buddy, there is no need for you to go to that difficulty. You may just emulate his behaviour to demonstrate that you are "as excellent as he is," but you cannot convince anyone that you are as wealthy as he is. Furthermore, if you put on these "airs," squander your time, money, and resources, your poor wife will be forced to wash her hands at home, buy her tea in two-ounce portions, and do everything else in moderation so that you may maintain your "appearances" and, in the end, mislead no one. On the other hand, Mrs. Julie may say that her next-door neighbor married Johnson for his money, and "everybody says so." She has a nice one-thousand-dollar camel's hair shawl, and she will make Julie get her an imitation one, and she will sit in a pew right next to her neighbor in church, in order to prove that she is her equal.

My good woman, you will not get ahead in the world, if your vanity and envy thus take the lead. In this country, where we believe the majority ought to rule, we ignore that principle in regard to fashion, and let a handful of people, calling themselves the aristocracy, run up a false standard of perfection, and in endeavoring to rise to that standard, we constantly keep ourselves poor; all the time digging away for the sake of outside appearances. How much wiser to declare that we will "control our out-go by our income, and lay aside something for a rainy day" and be a "law unto ourselves" People should be just as reasonable when it comes to making money as when it comes to any other topic. Similar causes lead to similar results. By travelling the path of least resistance, one cannot amass a wealth. No prophet is necessary to inform us that individuals who live within their means without considering a negative outcome in this life will never be financially independent.

Men and women accustomed to gratify every whim and caprice, will find it hard, at first, to cut down their various unnecessary expenses, and will feel it a great self-denial to live in a smaller house than they have been accustomed to, with less expensive furniture, less company, less costly clothing, fewer servants, a less number of balls, parties, theater-goings, carriage-ridings, pleasure excursions, cigar-smoking, liquor-drinking's, and other extravagances; but, after all, if they will try the plan of laying by a "nest-egg," or, in other words, a small sum of money, at interest or judiciously invested in land, they will be surprised at the pleasure to be derived from constantly adding to their little "pile," as well as from all the economical habits which are engendered by this course.

Adversity is less terrible than wealth, especially sudden riches. It's a well-known adage that "easy comes, easy goes." The unstoppable canker-worm that gnaws at the very core of a man's worldly riches, whether they be tiny or big, hundreds of millions, is a spirit of pride and vanity when it is allowed to have complete control. Many people, as soon as they start to flourish, extend their ideas and start spending on luxury. However, in a short period of time, their costs consume all of their money, and they end up bankrupt in their ludicrous attempts to maintain their appearances and create a "sensation."

A gentleman of fortune who says, that when he first began to prosper, his wife would have a new and elegant sofa. "That sofa," he says, "cost me thirty thousand dollars!" When the sofa reached the house, it was found necessary to get chairs to match; then sideboards, carpets and tables "to correspond" with them, and so on through the entire stock of furniture; when at last it was found that the house itself was quite too small and old-fashioned for the furniture, and a new one was built to correspond with the new purchases; "thus," added my friend, "summing up an outlay of thirty thousand dollars, caused by that single sofa, and saddling on me, in the shape of servants, equipage, and the necessary expenses attendant upon keeping up a fine 'establishment,' a yearly outlay of eleven thousand dollars, and a tight pinch at that: whereas, ten years ago, we lived with much more real comfort, because with much less care, on as many hundreds. The truth is," he continued, "that sofa would have brought me to inevitable bankruptcy, had not a most unexampled title to prosperity kept me above it, and had I not checked the natural desire to 'cut a dash'."

As the substratum of fortune and the base of enjoyment, good health is the cornerstone of success in life. When one is ill, one cannot amass wealth very successfully. He lacks drive, desire, and ambition. Of course, some people have poor health and can't change it; you can't expect these people to amass riches, but there are a lot of people in poor health who don't have to be that way.

How crucial it is that we learn about the rules of health, which are simply another way of saying the laws of nature, since sound health is the basis of success and enjoyment in life! The closer we abide by natural rules, the closer we are to being in good health, yet how many people completely disregard natural laws and go against them, sometimes even against their own natural inclinations? We should be aware that breaking nature's rules always carries a cost; the "sin of ignorance" is never overlooked in this regard. Even remorse won't stop a youngster from sticking their finger into the flames without realizing it would burn; as a result, they suffer. Many of our forefathers had extremely little knowledge of the ventilation concept. Whatever other "gin" they may have been familiar with, they did not know anything about oxygen, so they constructed their homes with tiny bedrooms that were seven by nine feet. These good old religious Puritans would lock themselves in one of these cells, say their prayers, and then go to bed. In the morning they would devoutly return thanks for the "preservation of their lives," during the night, and nobody had better reason to be thankful. Probably some big crack in the window, or in the door, let in a little fresh air, and thus saved them.

DON'T MISS YOUR OPPORTUNITY

The best strategy for a young guy just starting out in life is to choose a profession that appeals to his interests the most. In this aspect, parents and guardians are frequently far too careless. Fathers frequently make statements like, "I have five boys. Billy, John, Tom, and Dick will become clergymen, lawyers, doctors, and farmers, respectively. He then makes his way into town to look around and decide what to do with Sammy. Sammy, I see watch-making is a wonderful refined business; I suppose I will make you a goldsmith, he says when he gets home. He does this regardless of Sam's intelligence or inherent propensities.

Without a doubt, everyone of us was born for a good reason. Both our faces and our minds are incredibly diverse. Some people have a strong dislike to equipment, while others are born natural mechanics. If you gather a group of ten-year-old boys, you'll quickly notice that two or three of them are "whittling" away at some creative contraption, fiddling with locks or intricate equipment. Their father was unable to find a toy that would appeal to them like a puzzle when they were just five years old. Although the other eight or nine guys have varied aptitudes, they are both natural mechanics. I belong to the latter class; I never had the slightest love for mechanism; on the contrary, I have a sort of abhorrence for complicated machinery. I never had ingenuity enough to whittle a cider tap so it would not leak. I was never able to grasp the workings of a steam engine or create a pen that I could write with. The youngster might be able to disassemble and reassemble a watch after five or seven years of apprenticeship if a man tried to turn me into a watchmaker, but he would spend the rest of his life working hard and finding every justification to put off his tasks and waste time. He finds manufacturing watches disgusting.

Man cannot prosper unless he engages in the career that is most suited to his unique talent and that is meant for him by nature. I'm relieved to think that most people do discover their ideal profession. However, from the blacksmith on up (or down) to the preacher, we encounter individuals who have misunderstood their calling. You may have encountered attorneys, physicians, and clergymen who were more suited by nature for the anvil or the lap stone, as well as that amazing linguist known as the "educated blacksmith," who should have become a language instructor.

RIGHT PLACE, RIGHT TIME

You must be cautious while choosing the perfect place after acquiring the suitable spot. They claim it takes a genius to "know how to run a hotel," therefore you could have been made for the job. Even if you run a hotel flawlessly and can comfortably accommodate 500 people per day, the placement of your home in a remote community without access to either public transportation or a train would be your undoing.

It is similarly crucial that you avoid opening a firm in an industry where there are already sufficient resources to supply all demand.

AVOID DEBT LIKE THE PLAGUE

Young men starting in life should avoid running into debt. That's a given. There is scarcely anything else that drags a person down like debt. It is a slavish position to get ill, yet we find many a young man, hardly out of his "teens," running in debt (and yes, this has been going on for centuries as long as men and history could remember). He meets a chum and says, "Look at this: I have got trusted for a new suit of clothes." He seems to look upon the clothes as so much given to him; well, it frequently is so, but, if he succeeds in paying and then gets trusted again, he is adopting a habit which will keep him in poverty through life. *Debt robs a man of his self-respect, and makes him almost despise himself.*

Labouring for a dead horse is accurately described as "grunting and moaning and working for what he has eaten up or worn out" since when he is asked to pay, he has nothing to show for his money. I don't talk about business owners who buy and sell on credit or consumers who use credit to make a profit on a transaction.

Money is similar to fire in certain ways; it makes an amazing servant but a dreadful master. The worst type of enslavement will drag you down when it is dominating you and when interest is steadily stacking up against you. However, if you make money work for you, you will have the world's most loyal servant. There is no "eye-servant" here. Nothing inanimate or alive will function as dependably as money when it is invested and properly guarded. It functions day and night, in dry or rainy conditions.

Therefore, don't allow it go against you; if you do, you won't have any possibility of financial success in life.

SELF-RELIANCE IS REALLY JUST ANOTHER WORD FOR PERSEVERENCE.

A man must endure while on the correct road. This is important to note since there are certain people who are "born tired"—lazy by nature, lacking in self-reliance and tenacity. However, as Davy Crockett said, "This thing remember, when I am dead: Be sure you are right, then move ahead."

It is this go-ahead addiction, these resolves to not allow the horrors or the blues control you, that you must nurture in order to let your energies rest in the fight for independence.

How many have almost reached the goal of their ambition, but, losing faith in themselves, have relaxed their energies, and the golden prize has been lost forever. It is, no doubt, often true, as Shakespeare says:

"There is a tide in the affairs of men, Which, taken at the flood, leads on to fortune."

A braver hand will extend out in front of you and take the prize if you delay. A wise man once said, "He who deals with a slack hand becomes poor; but the hand of the diligent makes rich."

Self-reliance is occasionally just another term for perseverance. Many people are prone to seeing the worst aspects of life and borrowing problems. They are predisposed to being this way from birth. Then they seek counsel since they can't rely on themselves and will be carried along by one wind and blown by another. You shouldn't count on success until you can rely only on yourself.

Men who have met with pecuniary reverses, and absolutely committed suicide, because they thought they could never overcome their misfortune. But I have known others who have met more serious financial difficulties, and have bridged them over by simple perseverance, aided by a firm belief that they were doing justly, and that Providence would *"overcome evil with good."*

WHATEVER YOU DO, DO IT WITH ALL YOUR MIGHT

Work at it, if necessary, early and late, in season and out of season, not leaving a stone unturned, and never deferring for a single hour that which can be done just as well now. The old proverb is full of truth and meaning, "Whatever is worth doing at all, is worth doing well." Many a man acquires a fortune by doing his business thoroughly, while his neighbor remains poor for life, because he only half does it. Ambition, energy, industry, perseverance, are indispensable requisites for success in business.

Fortune never assists a man who does not help himself; it always favours the bold. It won't do to wait about as Mr. Micawber does for things to "turn up" in your life. Since idleness promotes ill habits and dresses a man in rags, one of two things often "turns up" for such men: the poorhouse or the prison. "I have found there is enough money in the world for all of us, provided it was equally split," the impoverished, wasteful vagrant tells the rich guy. "This must be done, and we would all be happy together."

"But," was the response, "if everybody was like you, it would be spent in two months, and what would you do then?"

"Oh! Divide again; keep dividing, of course!"

USE YOUR OWN PERSONAL EXERCISES AS A GUIDE.

The eyes of the employer are sometimes more valuable than a dozen workers' worth of hands.

An agent cannot, by nature, be as devoted to his employer as he is to himself. Many people who are employers may recall incidents where the greatest workers have missed crucial details that could not have slipped their own attention as an owner. No man has the right to assume that he will succeed in life until he fully comprehends his industry, and no one can fully comprehend his industry unless he learns it by personal application and experience. A man may be a manufacturer: he has got to learn the many details of his business personally; he will learn something every day, and he will find he will make mistakes nearly every day. And these very mistakes are helps to him in the way of experiences if he but heeds them. He will follow in the footsteps of the Yankee tin-peddler, who after being duped into believing his goods were of higher quality than they actually were, declared: "All right, there's a little information to be acquired every day; I will never be duped in that way again." Man buys his experience in this way, and if it isn't too expensive, it's the greatest sort.

Be careful and brave was one of the older Rothschild's maxims, which seems to contradict itself. Although it may appear like a contradiction in words, the saying really has a lot of insight. In actuality, it is a shortened version of what I previously said. It means "you must be cautious while making ideas, yet brave when carrying them out." A guy who is just cautious will never have the courage to seize the initiative and succeed, and a man who is only courageous is simply reckless and will inevitably fail. A man may go on "'change" and make fifty, or one hundred thousand dollars in speculating in stocks, at a single operation. But if he has simple boldness without caution, it is mere chance, and what he gains to-day he will lose to-morrow. You must have both the caution and the boldness, to ensure success.

There is no such thing as **LUCK** in the world. He may do so once in his life, but as far as pure luck is concerned, he is just as likely to lose it as to find it. There has never been a man who could go outside in the morning and discover a purse full of gold in the street today, another tomorrow, and so on, day after day. Similar causes lead to similar results. If a man uses the right strategies, "luck" will not stand in his way. There are reasons why he might not succeed, even if he might not be able to recognize them.

USE THE BEST TOOLS

Men should use caution while hiring staff to get the best. Realize that you can never have enough high-quality tools for your job, and that there is no tool you should hold in such high regard as live tools. If you find a good one, sticking with him is preferable to constantly changing. Every day he learns something new, and you gain from the experience he gains. If his habits are good and he remains faithful, he is the last man you want to lose and is worth more to you this year than he was last. If, as he becomes more valuable, he requests an outrageous wage raise, let him leave if you feel you can't function without him.

When and if you have such an employee, always fire him. This will both tell him that his position can be filled and will also make him useless if he believes he is indispensable and cannot be spared.

But you would want to keep him around so you could benefit from his experience. The brain is an essential component of a worker. Although there are bills up saying "Hands Wanted," "hands" are not very valuable without "heads."

Those men who have brains and experience are therefore the most valuable and not to be readily parted with; it is better for them, as well as yourself, to keep them, at reasonable advances in their salaries from time to time.

DON'T GET ABOVE YOUR BUSINESS

Instead of following their avocation and moving forward in their firm after completing their business training or apprenticeship, young men frequently tell lies about doing nothing. What is the use of studying my trade or profession unless I establish myself? they ask. "I have learnt my business, but I am not going to be a hireling."
"Do you have any initial capital?"
"No, but I'm having it anyhow."
How will you obtain it, I ask?

I'll tell you this privately: I have a wealthy, elderly aunt who is about to pass away. If she does not, I expect to find a wealthy, elderly man who will lend me a few thousand dollars to get started. I can succeed if I can only start with money.

There is no worse error than for a young guy to think that using borrowed money will help him achieve. Also observe that even in the 21st century, conversations of this nature are still common.

Why? Because every man's experience coincides with that of Mr. Astor, who said, "it was more difficult for him to accumulate his first thousand dollars, than all the succeeding millions that made up his colossal fortune." Money is good for nothing unless you know the value of it by experience. Give a boy twenty thousand dollars and put him in business, and the chances are that he will lose every dollar of it before he is a year older. Like buying a ticket in the lottery; and drawing a prize, it is "easy come, easy go." He does not know the value of it; nothing is worth anything, unless it costs effort. Without self-control, economy, patience, and perseverance, as well as starting with cash that you have not earned, you are unlikely to succeed in building up a significant amount of wealth. There is no class of individuals that is as unaccommodating in regards to dying as these wealthy old folks, and it is fortunate for the prospective heirs that it is so. Young men should be up and doing instead of "waiting for dead men's shoes."

"There is no royal road to learning," says the proverb, and I may say it is equally true, "there is no royal road to wealth." But I think there is a royal road to both. The road to learning is a royal one; the road that enables the student to expand his intellect and add every day to his stock of knowledge, until, in the pleasant process of intellectual growth, he is able to solve the most profound problems, to count the stars, to analyze every atom of the globe, and to measure the firmament this is a regal highway, and it is the only road worth traveling.

So in regards to wealth: go on in confidence, study the rules, and above all things, study human nature; for "the proper study of mankind is man," and you will find that while expanding the intellect and the muscles, your enlarged experience will enable you every day to accumulate more and more principal, which will increase itself by interest and otherwise, until you arrive at a state of independence. You will find, as a general thing, that the poor boys get rich and the rich boys get poor.

In this Republican country, the man makes the business. No matter whether he is a blacksmith, a shoemaker, a farmer, banker or lawyer, so long as his business is legitimate, he may be a gentleman. So, any "legitimate" business is a double blessing it helps the man engaged in it, and also helps others. The Farmer supports his own family, but he also benefits the merchant or mechanic who needs the products of his farm. The tailor not only makes a living by his trade, but he also benefits the farmer, the clergyman and others who cannot make their own clothing. But all these classes often may be gentlemen. The great ambition should be to excel all others engaged in the same occupation. The college-student who was about graduating, said to an old lawyer:

"I have not yet decided which profession I will follow. Is your profession full?"

"The basement is much crowded, but there is plenty of room up-stairs," was the witty and truthful reply.

In the top storey, there is no profession, trade, or calling that is overloaded. Wherever you locate the most honourable and wisest businessman or banker, or the greatest doctor, lawyer, or clergyperson, or the best shoemaker, carpenter, or anything else, you will discover that guy is most sought after and always has something to do. Americans as a whole are too superficial; they want to become wealthy quickly and don't always conduct business seriously and thoroughly enough. However, someone who excels in their field, as long as they have good habits and unquestionable integrity, is guaranteed to attract a lot of business and the wealth that follows naturally. Let your motto then always be "Excelsior," for by living up to it there is no such word as fail.

LEARN SOMETHING VALUE-ADDED

In these times of shifting fortunes, where one may be wealthy now but impoverished tomorrow, every father should insist that his children learn a practical skill or profession so that they will have something concrete to fall back on. Many people who have lost all of their resources due to an unforeseen circumstance might be spared from suffering by this arrangement.

LEAD WITH HOPE, BUT DON'T BE TOO VISIONARY

Because they have too much vision, many people are perpetually locked in poverty. They see every endeavour as a sure success, so they constantly switching from one firm to another, always in trouble, always "under the harrow." The idea of "counting the chickens before they are born" is a mistake that dates back a long time, yet it does not appear to get better with time.

BE SYSTEMATIC

Men should be systematic in their business. A person who does business by rule, having a time and place for everything, doing his work promptly, will accomplish twice as much and with half the trouble of him who does it carelessly and slipshod. By introducing system into all your transactions, doing one thing at a time, always meeting appointments with punctuality, you find leisure for pastime and recreation; whereas the man who only half does one thing, and then turns to something else, and half does that, will have his business at loose ends, and will never know when his day's work is done, for it never will be done. Of course, there is a limit to all these rules. We must try to preserve the happy medium, for there is such a thing as being too systematic. There are men and women, for instance, who put away things so carefully that they can never find them again. It is too much like the "red tape" formality at Washington, and Mr. Dickens' "Circumlocution Office,"—all theory and no result.

DON'T DISTRIBUTE YOUR POWERS

Engage in only one type of business and stay committed to it until you are successful or until your experience indicates that you should stop. One nail will usually finally be driven home with repeated hammering, allowing it to be clinched. A man's mind will continually offer valuable enhancements when his undivided concentration is focused on just one thing; these suggestions would otherwise escape him if his thinking was split between a dozen distinct topics. Many fortunes have been lost by men because they were involved in too many activities at once. The age-old advice to avoid juggling too many projects at once makes logic.

READ THE DAILY PAPERS

Always take a trustworthy newspaper, and thus keep thoroughly posted in regard to the transactions of the world. He who is without a newspaper is cut off from his species. In these days of the Internet, many important inventions and improvements in every branch of trade are being made, and he who don't consult the newspapers will soon find himself and his business left out in the cold Period.

DON'T INDORSE WITHOUT SECURITY

No man ought ever to indorse a note or become security, for any man, be it his father or brother, to a greater extent than he can afford to lose and care nothing about, without taking good security. Here is a man that is worth twenty thousand dollars; he is doing a thriving manufacturing or mercantile trade; you are retired and living on your money; he comes to you and says:

"You are aware that I am worth twenty thousand dollars, and don't owe a dollar; if I had five thousand dollars in cash, I could purchase a particular lot of goods and double my money in a couple of months; will you indorse my note for that amount?"

You reflect that he is worth twenty thousand dollars, and you incur no risk by endorsing his note; you like to accommodate him, and you lend your name without taking the precaution of getting security. Shortly after, he shows you the note with your endorsement cancelled, and tells you, probably truly, "that he made the profit that he expected by the operation," you reflect that you have done a good action, and the thought makes you feel happy. By and by, the same thing occurs again and you do it again; you have already fixed the impression in your mind that it is perfectly safe to indorse his notes without security.

PROMOTE YOUR BUSINESS

More or less, we all rely on the support of the general people. Lawyers, physicians, shoemakers, blacksmiths, artists, showmen, opera stage directors, railroad executives, and college teachers all conduct business with the general public. Those that conduct business with the general public need to take care that their products are worthwhile, real, and satisfying. When you find a product that you know will appeal to your audience and that, once they try it, will make them feel like they got their money's worth, let them know that you have found it. Be cautious to promote it in some way since it is obvious if a man has a very excellent item for sale and no one knows about it.

Where nearly everybody reads, and where newspapers are issued and circulated in editions of five thousand to two hundred thousand, it would be very unwise if this channel was not taken advantage of to reach the public in advertising. A newspaper goes into the family, and is read by wife and children, as well as the head of the home; hence hundreds and thousands of people may read your advertisement, while you are attending to your routine business. Many, perhaps, read it while you are asleep. The whole philosophy of life is, first "sow," then "reap." That is the way the farmer does; he plants his potatoes and corn, and sows his grain, and then goes about something else, and the time comes when he reaps. But he never reaps first and sows afterwards. This principle applies to all kinds of business, and to nothing more eminently than to advertising. If a man has a genuine article, there is no way in which he can reap more advantageously than by "sowing" to the public in this way. He must, of course, have a really good article, and one which will please his customers; anything spurious will not succeed permanently because the public is wiser than many imagine. Men and women are selfish, and we all prefer purchasing where we can get the most for our money and we try to find out where we can most surely do so.

BE POLITE AND KIND TO YOUR CUSTOMERS

Politeness and civility are the *best capital ever* invested in business. Large stores, gilt signs, flaming advertisements, will all prove unavailing if you or your employees treat your patrons abruptly. The truth is, *the more kind and liberal a man is the more generous will be the patronage bestowed upon him*. Like begets like. The man who gives the greatest amount of goods of a corresponding quality for the least sum (still reserving for himself a profit) will generally succeed best in the long run. This brings us to the golden rule, "*As ye would that men should do to you, do ye also to them*" and they will do better by you than if you always treated them as if you wanted to get the most you could out of them for the least return.

Men who drive sharp bargains with their customers, acting as if they never expected to see them again, will not be mistaken. They will never see them again as customers.

BE CHARITABLE

Of course, men should be charitable, **because it is a duty and a pleasure**. But even as a matter of policy, if you possess no higher incentive, you will find that the liberal man will command patronage, while the sordid, uncharitable miser will be avoided.

Solomon says: *"There is that scattered and yet increased; and there is that withhold more than meet, but it tended to poverty."* Of course, the only true charity is that which is from the heart. The finest kind of charity is to lend a hand to those who are eager to lend a hand to themselves. Promiscuous almsgiving without considering the applicant's value is wrong in every way. But the sort that disperse but grow is the kind that discreetly seeks out and helps others who are battling for themselves. Don't, however, get into the notion that some people have that feeding the needy with a prayer or blessing rather than food will satisfy them. Making Christians is simpler with a full stomach than an empty one.

PRESERVE YOUR INTEGRITY

Integrity is more precious than diamonds or rubies. This advice was not only atrociously wicked, but it was the very essence of stupidity: It was as much as to say if you find it difficult to obtain money honestly, you can easily get it dishonestly. **Not to know that the most difficult thing in life is to make money dishonestly!** Not to know that our prisons are full of men who attempted to follow this advice; not to understand that no man can be dishonest, without soon being found out, and that when his lack of principle is discovered, nearly every avenue to success is closed against him forever. The public very properly shun all whose integrity is doubted. No matter how polite and pleasant and accommodating a man may be, none of us dare to deal with him if we suspect "false weights and measures." Strict honesty, not only lies at the foundation of all success in life (financially), but in every other respect.

To get rich, is not always equivalent to being successful. *"There are many rich poor men,"* while there are many others, honest and devout men and women, who have never possessed so much money as some rich persons squander in a week, but who are nevertheless really richer and happier than any man can ever be while he is a transgressor of the higher laws of his being.

Money itself, when used properly, is not only a "handy thing to have in the house," but it also provides the satisfaction of blessing our race by allowing its possessor to increase the scope of human happiness and human influence. There is no doubt that an excessive love of money may be and is "the root of all evil," but money itself is not only a "handy thing to have in the house." The desire for riches is almost universal, and no one can argue that it is not admirable as long as the owner accepts their obligations and uses their fortune to benefit humanity.

The history of acquiring wealth, which is commerce, is a history of civilization, and wherever trade has flourished most, there, too, have art and science produced the noblest fruits. In fact, as a general thing, money-getters are the benefactors of our race. To them, in a great measure, are we indebted for our institutions of learning and of art, our academies, colleges and churches. It is no argument against the desire for, or the possession of wealth, to say that there are sometimes misers who hoard money only for the sake of hoarding and who have no higher aspiration than to grasp everything which comes within their reach. As we have sometimes hypocrites in religion, and demagogues in politics, so there are occasionally misers among, money-getters. These, however, are only exceptions to the general rule.

To all men and women: make money honestly, and not otherwise, for Shakespeare has truly said, *"He that wants money, means, and content, is without three good friends."*

REMOVE BLAB

Men sometimes have the stupid tendency of divulging their company secrets. If they are successful, they enjoy showing their neighbours how it was done. Nothing is gained through this, and quite frequently, quite a bit is lost. Keep your earnings, aspirations, ambitions, and objectives to yourself. And both writing and verbal communication should follow this rule.

Businessmen must compose letters, but they must be cautious about what they include. Be extra cautious and keep it a secret if you are losing money, otherwise your reputation may suffer.

www.ingramcontent.com/pod-product-compliance
Lightning Source LLC
Chambersburg PA
CBHW080438220526
45465CB00009B/3340